CONSERVATIVE

BOOK

This edition published in 2008

10 9 8 7 6 5 4 3 2 1

A CIP catalogue record for this book is available from the British Library

ISBN 978-1-85375-681-8

Project Editor: Martin Corteel
Designer: Paul Chattaway
Production: Lisa French

Printed in Singapore

THE LITTLE CONSERVATIVE BOOK

Compiled by **Aubrey Malone**

PRION

Introduction

It has been said that politics is the second oldest profession in the world – and that it bears more than one resemblance to the first. With this in mind I've been delving into the archives and have come up with a selection of generally acerbic soundbites by and about those who have professed to run the country, even as they were in the process of opening their collective mouths to change feet.

There are also, shock horror, some idealistic prognostications uttered by legends of the Conservative Party, both dead and living. Many of these hark back to the past, which may tell us everything we want to know about the state of the nation today, or our dystopian fears for its future. There's also internecine squabbling, grandiose outrage, insightful whimsy and bite-sized chunks of post-Churchillian hyperbole, undercut by some revisionist asides. But then hindsight is always 20/20, isn't it?

The term "little" attached to "Conservative" may to some appear incongruous. Conservatives may be physically challenged but psychologically speaking they tend to walk (and talk) tall, usually believing they occupy the high moral ground if not the high physical one. Nonetheless, I have endeavoured to shoehorn a generation of historical – and often hysterical – utterances into these pages as a kind of freeze-frame photograph of the century just gone, and the one recently begun. Sample it at your discretion.

Aubrey Malone
April 2008

"Mr Speaker, I withdraw. Half the Cabinet are not asses."

Benjamin Disraeli after being asked to withdraw his allegation that half the Cabinet were asses

“Everyone in public life should be arrested at least once.”

Alan Clark

“The cocks may crow, but it’s the hen that lays the egg.”

Margaret Thatcher

"The Conservative establishment has always treated women as nannies, grannies and fannies."

Teresa Gorman

"Greater love hath no man than this, that he lay down his friends for his life."

Jeremy Thorpe after Harold Macmillan's multiple sacking of members of his Cabinet in 1962

“I have often found that the man who trusts nobody is apt to be the kind of man nobody trusts.”

Harold Macmillan

"A *deux* he is delightful, clever, funny, observant, drily cynical. But get him anywhere near "display mode" and he might as well have a corncob up his arse"

Alan Clark on Douglas Hurd

"I am prepared to meet my Maker. Whether my Maker is prepared for the great ordeal of meeting me is another matter."

Winston Churchill shortly before he died

"I have so many skeletons in the cupboard I can hardly shut the door."

Alan Clark

"Tony Blair is a mixture of Harry Houdini and a greased piglet. Nailing him is like trying to pin jelly to a wall."

Boris Johnson

"I was born in Rotherham. Around where I lived, people thought a Conservative was something you spread on your toast."

William Hague

“Blair goes one way, Brown goes the other way, and bang goes the third way.”

Michael Howard

“I haven’t got the figure for jeans.”

Margaret Thatcher

"There's no smoke without mud being flung around."

Edwina Currie

"That would be difficult."

Edward Heath replying to Margaret Thatcher when she asked him to sit on her right for a photograph

"Those who say I am not in agreement with the policy are, rightly or wrongly, quite wrong."

William Whitelaw on immigration

"We mustn't pre-judge the past."

William Whitelaw

"The great she-elephant, she who must be obeyed, the Catherine the Great of Finchley."

Denis Healey on Margaret Thatcher

"What can you do with a man who looks like a female llama surprised while bathing?"

Winston Churchill on Clement Attlee

"The Labour Party is going around stirring up apathy."

William Whitelaw

"The Liberal Democrat leader has gone in a few short weeks from 'Have I Got News For You' to 'I'm Sorry, I Haven't Got a Clue.' "

William Hague on Charles Kennedy

"Gordon Brown bases his politics on the Dolly Parton School of Economics – an unbelievable figure blown out of all proportion, with no visible means of support."

Kenneth Clarke

"When I was a young man I was told that the two occupational hazards of the Palace of Varieties [Westminster] were alcohol and adultery. The hurroosh that follows the intermittent revelation of the sexual goings-on of an unlucky MP has convinced me that the only safe pleasure for a parliamentarian is a bag of boiled sweets."

Julian Critchley

"No one would have remembered the Good Samaritan if he'd only had good intentions. He had money as well."

Margaret Thatcher

"An entire family of divorcees and they're head of the Church of England. It's going to make the person out there wonder if it's all worth it."

Jeffrey Archer on the Royal Family in 1992

"When I was younger I made it a rule never to take a strong drink before lunch. It is now my rule never to do so before breakfast."

Winston Churchill

"She cannot see an institution without hitting it with her handbag."

Julian Critchley on Margaret Thatcher

“We are not at war with Egypt. We are in armed conflict.”

Sir Anthony Eden

“Bringing up children on your own is very difficult even where there are two parents.”

Virginia Bottomley

"A great party is not to be brought down because of a scandal by a woman of easy virtue and a proved liar."

Lord Hailsham on the Profumo affair

"The amateur in politics is the person who's always sure he knows the result of the next General Election."

Enoch Powell

"I thought he was a young man of promise, but it appears he was a young man of promises."

A.J. Balfour on Winston Churchill

"I'm worried about that young man. He's getting awfully bossy."

Margaret Thatcher on Tony Blair in February 1999

“If John Major was drowning his whole life would pass before him … and he wouldn't be in it.”

Dave Allen

"Gordon Brown has the charisma of a coffin lid."

Michael Portillo

"Margaret Thatcher sounds like the Book of Revelations read out over a railway station public address system by a headmistress of a certain age wearing calico knickers."

Clive James

"I don't understand Cool Britannia. I believe in Rule Britannia."

Margaret Thatcher

“A Foreign Secretary is forever poised between a cliché and an indiscretion.”

Harold Macmillan

"There are three things in this world you can do nothing about: Getting AIDS, getting clamped and running out of Château Lafite 45."

Alan Clark

“You know what they say: Don’t get mad, get angry.”

Edwina Currie

"A statesman wants courage and vision, but after six months he wants first, second, third and all the time – patience."

Stanley Baldwin

"When I am abroad I always make it a rule never to attack the government of my country. I make up for lost time when I come home."

Winston Churchill

"History is littered with wars which everybody knew would never happen."

Enoch Powell

"I wasn't even in the Index."

Edwina Currie taking umbrage at the fact that she wasn't mentioned in John Major's autobiography

“A politician needs the ability to foretell what is going to happen tomorrow, next week, next month and next year. And afterwards to explain why it didn't.”

Winston Churchill

"It is exciting when you have a real crisis on your hands when you have spent half your political life dealing with humdrum issues like the environment."

Margaret Thatcher

"If Gladstone fell into the Thames, that would be a misfortune. If anyone pulled him out, that, I suppose, would be a calamity."

Benjamin Disraeli

"There are two problems in my life. The political ones are insoluble and the economic ones are incomprehensible."

Sir Alec Douglas-Home

“There’s nothing that improves the mood of the party as the imminent execution of a senior colleague.”

Alan Clark

"It has been said that democracy is the worst form of government, except for all the other ones."

Winston Churchill

"Music means everything to me when I'm alone. And it's the best way of getting that bloody man Wilson out of my hair."

Edward Heath

"Stanley Baldwin occasionally stumbled across the truth, but hastily picked himself up and hurried on as if nothing had happened."

Winston Churchill

"With the publication of his private papers in 1952, Earl Haig committed suicide 25 years after his death."

Lord Birkenhead

“A Conservative government is organized hypocrisy.”

Benjamin Disraeli

Bessie Braddock
You're drunk,
Prime Minister.

Winston Churchill
Indeed I am. But you're ugly.
And tomorrow I shall be sober.

“I would rather be an opportunist and float than go to the bottom with my principles round my neck.”

Stanley Baldwin

"I do not wear a bleeper. I can't speak in soundbites. I refuse to repeat slogans. I hate focus groups. I absolutely hate image consultants."

Kenneth Clarke

“John Major's self-control in cabinet was rigid. The most angry thing he would ever do was throw down his pencil.”

Gillian Shephard

“A communist is like a crocodile. When it opens its mouth you can’t tell whether it’s trying to smile or preparing to eat you up.”

Winston Churchill

"Labour are pushing lies through our doorstep."

Lord Waldegrave

"The Conservative Party, in time, always forgives those who were wrong. Indeed, in time it even forgives those who were right."

Iain MacLeod

"Every Labour government in my lifetime has run out of money."

Kenneth Clarke

"Unfortunately, monetarism, like Marxism, suffered the only fate that, for a theory, is worse than death: it was put into practice."

Ian Gilmour

“Disloyalty is the secret weapon of the Tory Party.”

Julian Critchley

“I have the most corny CV possible. It goes: Eton, Oxford, Conservative Research Department, Treasury, Home Office, Carlton TV and then Conservative MP.”

David Cameron

“Not only is he a bore; he bores for England.”

Malcolm Muggeridge on Anthony Eden

"Something that I was not aware had happened suddenly turned out not to have happened."

John Major giving evidence to the Scott Inquiry in 1994

"I never forgive but I always forget."

A.J. Balfour

“A man with the vision of an eagle but with a blind spot in one eye.”

Andrew Bonar Law on Lord Birkenhead

“I can trust my husband not to fall asleep on a public platform. And he usually claps in the right places.”

Margaret Thatcher

“Is it not the case that those found guilty of fraud are the only people left in the Labour Party with genuine convictions?”

William Hague

"Like most Chief Whips, he knew who the shits were."

Alan Clark on Michael Jopling

“If people want a sense of purpose they should get it from their archbishops. They should not hope to get it from their politicians.”

Harold Macmillan

"I hope Mrs Thatcher will go to the end of the [twentieth] century looking like Queen Victoria."

Norman Tebbit

"Double talk is his mother tongue. He is a man whose vision is limited to tomorrow's headlines."

Iain MacLeod on Harold Wilson

"Neil Kinnock's speeches go on for so long because he has nothing to say so he has no way of knowing when he's finished saying it."

John Major

“I’ve always had a frustrated desire to run a hotel.”

Edward Heath

"I wonder if Neil Kinnock exists at all, or if he's some plastic puppet squeezed into shape by his PR experts and trade union leaders, or whoever bullied him last."

Norman Tebbit

"A big cat detained briefly in a poodle parlour, sharpening her claws on the velvet."

Matthew Parris describing Margaret Thatcher in the House of Lords

Nancy Astor
If I were your wife I would
put poison in your coffee.

Winston Churchill
And if I were your husband
I'd drink it.

"I oppose the plan to reform the House of Lords. I will be sad if I look down after my death and don't see my son asleep on the same benches on which I slept."

Lord Onslow

“No woman will in my time be prime minister.”

Margaret Thatcher in 1969

"Whenever I want a good read I get one of Jeffrey Archer's novels and stand on it so I can reach the good books."

Steven Norris

"It was a bitter irony that our first woman prime minister was Thatcher – a case of a man in a frock."

Edwina Currie

“We cannot ignore the price that unemployment today is exacting from the failures of the past. I know about these things. I grew up in the Thirties with an unemployed father. He did not riot. He got on his bike and looked for work.”

Norman Tebbit

“The best argument against democracy is a five-minute conversation with the average voter.”

Winston Churchill

“I’m down to my last hundred million.”

Jeffrey Archer explaining why he sold his Andy Warhol painting

"After a few months learning geography, now I've got to learn arithmetic."

Harold Macmillan on moving from the Foreign Office to the Treasury

"Any woman who understands the problem of running a home will be nearer to understanding the problem of running a country."

Margaret Thatcher

"All political lives, unless they are cut off in midstream at a happy juncture, end in failure."

Enoch Powell

"I do not believe that one person's poverty is caused by another's wealth."

Michael Howard

“At an election an old woman in the crowd called me a bastard. I replied, ‘Mother, I told you to stay at home.’ ”

F. E. Smith

"Dead birds don't fall out of nests."

Winston Churchill after being advised in old age that his flies were undone

“There are no true friends in politics. We’re all sharks, circling and waiting for traces of blood to appear in the water.”

Alan Clark

"Margaret Thatcher and Ted Heath both have a great vision. The difference is that Thatcher has a vision that Britain will one day be great again, and Heath has a vision that one day Heath will be great again."

Robert Jones

"I would rather consult my valet than the Conservative conference."

A.J. Balfour

"Running a country is like playing the organ. You have to use all the stops, pull out one and pull back the other. It is not like playing the penny whistle."

Harold Macmillan

"There's as much chance of my becoming Prime Minister as there is of finding Elvis on Mars, or my being decapitated by a frisbee, or being reincarnated as an olive."

Boris Johnson

“I’m drawing a line under the sand.”

John Major on the Maastricht Treaty in 1992

"The difference between Maggie Thatcher and Joan of Arc is that Thatcher only hears her own voice."

Peter Ustinov

“The trend in the rise in unemployment is downward.”

Gillian Shephard

"Michael Howard has something of the night about him."

Ann Widdecombe

"Being an MP feeds your vanity and starves your self-respect."

Matthew Parris

"If Her Majesty stood for Parliament, if the Tory Party had any sense and made her its leader instead of that grammar school twit Heath, us Tories, mate, would win every election we went in for"

Johnny Speight's **Alf Garnett** in the TV programme "Till Death Us Do Part"

"I will never forget the '81 – or was it the '82? – honours list."

Julian Critchley

"I am not a product of privilege. I am a product of opportunity."

Edward Heath

"In politics if you want anything said, ask a man. If you want anything done, ask a woman."

Margaret Thatcher

"We have become a grandmother."

Margaret Thatcher

"If all we needed to govern the country was someone who repeated everything we'd said before, we could have bought a parrot."

William Hague expressing his disgruntlement at the appointment of Tony Blair as prime minister in a Conservative Party speech in Blackpool on October 7, 1999

"John Prescott looks like a terrifying mixture of Hannibal Lecter and Terry Scott."

Gyles Brandreth

"Since the dawn of time every politician has been torn between a wish to say something memorable and a terror of saying something which is remembered."

Matthew Parris

"Neil Kinnock walked backwards into socialism as the penniless man walked backwards into the cinema, in the hope that the attendant would think he was leaving it."

Nigel Lawson

"I don't mind how much ministers talk as long as they do what I say."

Margaret Thatcher

"I am humble enough to recognize that I have made mistakes, but politically astute enough to know that I have forgotten what they are."

Michael Heseltine

“How dare he tell me what to do when he has a circumference to rival the equator.”

Ann Widdecombe after Frank Dobson, then Health Minister, advised her to take more fibre to reduce her weight in 1998

"He who wields the knife never wears the crown."

Michael Heseltine

"It needs to be said that the poor are poor because they don't have enough money."

Sir Keith Joseph

“New Labour doesn’t do candour. Mr Blair will find humility when the hippopotomus finds grace.”

Matthew Parris

“I do not often attack the Labour Party. They do it so well themselves.”

Edward Heath

“I wouldn’t say she’s open-minded on the Middle East so much as empty-headed. She probably thinks Sinai is the plural of sinus.”

Jonathan Aitken on Margaret Thatcher

"The dreadful truth is that when people come to see their MP they have run out of better ideas."

Boris Johnson

"He behaves like an agitated parrot with constipation."

John Major on Frank Dobson

“I don’t blame anyone, except perhaps all of us.”

William Whitelaw

Reporter
Who wears the pants in your house?

Denis Thatcher
I do, but I also wash and iron them.

"If Roland Rat were appointed to Northern Ireland I would tell people to work with him, but I would still point out that he was a rat."

William Hague after Peter Mandelson was appointed Northern Ireland Secretary in 1999

“In a long experience of politics I have never found that criticism is ever inhibited by ignorance.”

Harold Macmillan

"Memorial services are the cocktail parties of the geriatric set."

Harold Macmillan

"Suicide is a real threat to health in a modern society."

Virginia Bottomley

"Robin Cook is the only Foreign Secretary in 700 years who has more trouble at home than he has abroad. But don't mock. One day his looks will go."

John Major

“Sustainable growth is growth that is sustainable.”

John Major

"I think sometimes the prime minister should be intimidating. There's not much point in being a weak, floppy thing in the chair, is there?"

Margaret Thatcher

“The duty of an opposition is very simple – to oppose everything and propose nothing.”

Lord Derby, 1841

"When you're abroad you're a statesman. When you're at home you're just a politician."

Harold Macmillan

“If the angel Gabriel had stood with the name of Winston Churchill, Ken would still have won.”

Jeffrey Archer on Ken Livingstone becoming mayor of London in 2000

"Megaphone diplomacy leads to a dialogue of the deaf."

Geoffrey Howe

"Politicians who complain about the media are like ships' captains who complain about the sea."

Enoch Powell

"I must follow them.
I am their leader."

A.J. Balfour

"He is one of those orators of whom it was well said, 'Before they get up they do not know what they are going to say; when they are speaking they do not know what they are saying; and when they have sat down they do not know what they have said."

Winston Churchill on Lord Charles Beresford in a House of Commons speech on December 20, 1912

"Every prime minister needs a Willie."

Margaret Thatcher's unwitting pun when referring to William Whitelaw at a retirement dinner in his honour

“Above any other position of eminence, that of prime minister is filled by fluke.”

Enoch Powell

“I have the thermometer in my mouth and I’m listening to it all the time.”

William Whitelaw using an unfortunate choice of words in October 1974 during an election campaign

"We now have the worst of both worlds – not just inflation on the one side or stagnation on the other, but both of them together. We have a sort of 'stagflation' situation."

Iain MacLeod

"Everybody is always in favour of general economy and particular expenditure."

Anthony Eden

"The Liberal Democrats are not just empty. They are a void within a vacuum, surrounded by a vast inanation."

Boris Johnson

“The Tory Party only panics in a crisis.”

Iain MacLeod

"That's Anthony for you – half mad baronet, half beautiful woman."

R. A. Butler on the colourful parentage of Anthony Eden

"Politics are almost as exciting as war, and quite as dangerous. In war you can only be killed once, but in politics many times."

Winston Churchill

“It is rather like sending your opening batsman to the crease only for them to find the moment the first balls are bowled that their bats have been broken before the game by the team captain.”

Geoffrey Howe's resignation speech as deputy prime minister on November 13, 1990, outlining his difficulties with Margaret Thatcher

“I think you have to be very careful when you say ‘God is on my side’. I much prefer to say, ‘I am on God’s side.’ ”

Ann Widdecombe

"A politician should always appear stupider than he is."

Nigel Lawson

"Humming, Hawing and Hesitation are the three graces of contemporary parliamentary oratory."

Julian Critchley

"I want to talk about the future. He was the future once."

David Cameron sends his opening salvo across the despatch box to Tony Blair

Sources

P6 *The Little Book of Leadership Gaffes,* David MacFarlane, 2005; **p7** attrib.; **p8** *The Sunday Times*, April 9, 1989; **p9** *The Times*, November 14, 1998; **p10** *The General Election of 1964,* D.E. Butler; **p11** *The Observer*, December 22, 1963; **p12** *Alan Clark Diaries*, 1993; **p13** *True Confessions*, Jon Winokur, 2004; **p14** *The Book of Political Bollocks*, 2004; **p15** *Brit Wit*, Susie Jones, 2004; **p16** *The Guardian*, October 11, 1997; **p17** *I Wish I'd Said That*, Ned Sherrin, 2004; **p18** *True Confessions*, Jon Winokur, 2004; **p19** *The Book of Political Bollocks*, 2004; **p20** *The Times*, April 24, 1999; **p21** *On the House*, Simon Hoggart, 1981; **p22** *The Times*, July 2, 1999; **p23** *The Observer*, March 4, 1984; **p24** Winston Churchill 1944; **p25** *The Observer*, May 1, 1983; **p26** *The Sunday Times*, November 21, 1999; **p27** *Ultimate Wit*, Des MacHale, 2002; **p28** *The Listener*, June 10, 1982; **p29** *The Observer*, 1980; **p30** *Collins Quotation Finder*, 1999; **p31** Winston Churchill; **p32** *The Times*, June 21, 1982; **p33** *The Observer*, November 4, 1956; **p34** *The Book of Political Bollocks*, 2004; **p35** *The Pendulum Years* by Bernard Levin; **p36** House of Commons speech, 1981; **p37** *Winston Churchill, Vol. 2*, Randolph Churchill; **p38** Margaret Thatcher, February 1999; **p39** *The Independent*, March 1993; **p40** *Grumpy Old Wit*, Rosemarie Jarski, 2007; **p41** Clive James; **p42** *The Observer*, 1998; **p43** *Newsweek*, April 30, 1956; **p44** *The Book of Political Bollocks*, 2004; **p45** *Colemanballs 6, Private Eye,* 1992; **p46** Plymouth speech, October 26, 1923; **p47** House of Commons speech, April 18, 1947; **p48** *The Observer*, October 22, 1967; **p49** *The Times*, September 28, 2002; **p50** *Churchill Wit*, B. Adler, 1965); **p51** speech to the Scottish Conservative Party, May 14, 1982; **p52** *The Fine Art of Political Wit*, Leon Harris (ed.),1965: **p53** *The Times*, January 9, 1964; **p54** *Alan Clark Diaries*, entry for July 13, 1990; **p55** House of Commons speech, November 11, 1947; **p56** *The Abuse of Power*, James Margach, 1978; **p57** *Put Downs*, Laura Ward, 2004; **p58** *Men and Power*, 1956;

p59 *Hansard*, March 17, 1845; **p60** famous exchange, possibly apocryphal; **p61** *True Confessions*, Jon Winokur, 2004; **p62** *New Statesman*, February 12, 1999; **p63** *The Sunday Times*, November 21, 1999; **p64** *Read My Quips*, Vernon McLellan, 1991; **p65** *Colmanballs 6, Private Eye*, 1992; **p66** *The Spectator*, February 21, 1964; **p67** *The Guardian*, April 25, 2005; **p68** *Dancing With Dogma*, 1993; **p69** *The Observer*, November 11, 1990; **p70** *Grumpy Old Wit*, Rosemarie Jarski, 2007; **p71** Malcolm Muggeridge; **p72** evidence to the Scott Inquiry, 1994; **p73** *The Conservative Party*, R. Blake, 1970; **p74** *The Guinness Dictionary of Poisonous Quotes*, Colin Jarman, 1991; **p75** *The Observer*, August 20, 1978; **p76** *Ultimate Wit*, Des MacHale, 2002; **p77** *Alan Clark Diaries*, entry for June 17, 1987; **p78** *The Life of Politics*, Henry Fairlie, 1968; **p79** *The Observer*, May 17, 1987; **p80** *The Mammoth Book of Insults*, Geoff Tibballs, 2007; **p81** *Scorn*, Matthew Parris (ed.), 1994; **p82** *True Confessions*, Jon Winokur, 1992; **p83** *The Official Candidates' Book of Political Insults*; **p84** *The Book of Great One-Liners*, 2006; **p85** *Glitter and Gold*, Consuelo Vanderbilt Balsan 1952; **p86** *The Times*, October 1998; **p87** *Uncle John's Colossal Collection of Quotable Quotes*, 2004; **p88** *Scorn*, Matthew Parris (ed.), 1994; **p89** *The Book of Political Bollocks*, 2004; **p90** *The Daily Telegraph*, October 16, 1981; **p91** *Brit Wit*, Susie Jones, 2004; **p92** *The Guardian*, September 28, 1998; **p93** *A Prime Minister on Prime Ministers*, 1977; **p94** *The Observer*, May 8, 1979; **p95** *Joseph Chamberlain*, 1977; **p96** *The Book of Political Bollocks*, 2004; **p97** *Ready Wit*, Des MacHale, 2004; **p98** *The Lyttelton Letters, Vol. 2*; **p99** *Alan Clark Diaries*, November 30, 1990; **p100** speech at Conservative Party Conference, 1981; **p101** *Scorn*, Matthew Parris (ed.), 1994; **p102** Harold Macmillan in 1974; **p103** *Great British Wit*, Rosemarie Jarski, 2005; **p104** *The Dictionary of Regrettable Quotations*, 1999; **p105** *Quotable Ustinov*, 1995; **p106** *The Book of Political Bollocks*, 2004; **p107** *The Mammoth Book of Comic Quotes*, Geoff Tibballs, 2004; **p108** *The Times*, 1994; **p109** "Till Death Us Do Part";

p110 *Colemanballs 6, Private Eye*, 1992; **p111** *True Confessions*, Jon Winokur, 2004; **p112** *People*, September 15, 1975; **p113** *The Times*, March 4, 1989; **p114** Conservative Party speech in Blackpool, October 7, 1999; **p115** *The Mammoth Book of Insults*, Geoff Tibballs, 2007; **p116** *Read My Lips*, Matthew Parris, 1998; **p117** *The Official Candidates' Book of Political Insults*; **p118** *The Observer*, January 27, 1980; **p119** *Great British Wit*, Rosemarie Jarski, 2005; **p120** Ann Widdecombe, 1998; **p121** *New Society*, February 14, 1986; **p122** Sir Keith Joseph; **p123** *Great British Wit*, Rosemary Jarski, 2005; **p124** *The Observer*, June 10, 1973; **p125** *The Dictionary of Regrettable Quotations*; **p126** *Great British Wit*, Rosemarie Jarski, 2005; **p127** *The Mammoth Book of Insults*, Geoff Tibballs, 2007; **p128** *The Dictionary of Regrettable Quotations*, 1999; **p129** *The Book of Great One-Liners*, Jenny Hunter, 2006; **p130** William Hague, 1999; **p131** *The Observer*, December 29, 1963; **p132** *Macmillan*, Alistair Horne, 1989; **p133** *The Book of Political Bollocks*, 2004; **p134** *Wit Rides Again*, Des MacHale, 2000; **p135** *Colemanballs 6, Private Eye*, 1992; **p136** BBC1's "The Thatcher Years", October 21, 1993; **p137** *Dictionary of Cynical Quotations*, Jonathon Green, 1994; **p138** *The Observer*, July 28, 1963; **p139** *The Independent on Sunday*, May 7, 2000; **p140** *The Observer*, September 29, 1985; **p141** attrib.; **p142** *Mr Balfour*, E. Raymond, 1938 (also attributed to Andrew Bonar Law); **p143** House of Commons speech on December 20, 1912; **p144** Michael Cockerell in *The Guardian*; **p145** *The Observer*, March 8, 1987; **p146** William Whitelaw 1974; **p147** speech in the House of Commons, 1965; **p148** *The Observer*, June 17, 1956; **p149** *The Mammoth Book of Comic Quotes*, Geoff Tibballs (Ed), 2004; **p150** Iain MacLeod; **p151** *Anthony Eden*, David Carlton, 1981; **p152** *I Wish I'd Said That*, Ned Sherrin, 2004; **p153** *The Conflict of Loyalty*, 1994; **p154** *In the Psychiatrist's Chair III*, Anthony Clare, 1998; **p155** *The View from Number 11*, 1993; **p156** Julian Critchley; **p157** *The Observer,* May 25, 2008.